C000262782

LEEDS

in the Eighties and Nineties

LEEDS

in the Eighties and Nineties

First published in Great Britain in 2011 by The Derby Books Publishing Company Limited, 3 The Parker Centre, Derby, DE21 4SZ

All the photographs in this book are available to buy by visiting the YEP website or by the following telephone number: 0113 2388360.

ISBN 978-1-85983-992-8
Printed and bound by Melita Press, Malta

Contents

Foreword

LEEDS is a city which rarely stands still.

Every day, somewhere in this part of Yorkshire, something is changing.

Yet, even in the Leeds history of hustle and bustle, the decades of the 1980s and the 1990s stand out as years of transformation. It's easy to forget that, as the city moved into the eighties, there were many working-age adults who'd served in World War Two. Many people recalled living through the tough times of the twenties and thirties, and war and post-war rationing. Gas lighting, trams and smog were gone, but in 1980 Leeds had many tens of thousands of people employed in heavy industry, and coal mines were just down the road.

The photographs in this latest *Yorkshire Evening Post* book cover twenty years in which the city we now see began to come together. They were decades of development.

Among the buildings which went up were Quarry House, standing on the site of the flats which have featured so prominently in earlier *Yorkshire Evening Post* books, the White Rose Centre to the south of the city, Leeds City Bus Station and Number One City Square: the office block which still dominates the view from the train station.

The Royal Armouries appeared and there are pictures of the M1/M621 link road which cut through some of the older suburbs, a boon for drivers but rarely a benefit for the communities divided by it.

There are also photographs of well-known businesses, such as the restaurant Bibis, pictured in Mill Hill looking rather less glamorous than in its current incarnation, and the Merrion Centre when it was new.

The early nineties are years which football fans look back on with considerable nostalgia – Leeds United took the First Division title in 1992, the best team in the land. Several photographs show the team from that great 1991–92 season, resplendent in their *Yorkshire Evening Post*-sponsored strip. Included are images of the open-top bus tour of Leeds when the team shared their triumph with vast numbers of supporters who packed city centre streets.

Many of the names in the squad of that year are still as familiar to fans now as any there have ever been.

Leeds is a vibrant, never-sleeping city. The eighties and nineties helped make it what it is today. Those years are slipping into history. I hope you enjoy looking at this book of photographs taken by Yorkshire Evening Post photographers and, if you were in our city in the decades at the end of the twentieth century, wonderful memories are brought back by them.

Paul Napier
Editor
Yorkshire Evening Post

The 1980s

Leeds, 27 January 1980. Firemen tackle a blaze at Waring and Guillow, Land's Lane Entrance.

Leeds, Oakwood, 5 January 1980. A BBC film crew clambered into a skip piled high with waste paper to the amazement of shoppers in a nearby Leeds supermarket. The crew were filming the monthly waste paper collection in the car park of Safeways, Roundhay Road, Oakwood, for a BBC *Horizon* documentary to be screened on 3 March. The picture shows Mr Pat McCabe, representing the Irish community in Leeds, and a member of the Leeds Recycling Committee, being filmed by the BBC crew at Safeways.

Leeds, 25 August 1980. Just some of the huge crowd at Leeds Gala.

Leeds, 19 February 1980. Catch a Can appeal at Safeways, Oakwood. In only three weeks, 17 cwts of cans have been collected by the public for the Catch a Can appeal in the skip at Safeways, Oakwood. Here, at the Reclamation Centre, Meanwood Road, Leeds, members of the British Trust Conservation Volunteers, Environmental Health Department and the project manager from can manufacturers will count and analyse the cans to find the ratio between food and drink cans and also to find how many to the ton. Here, conservationist Craig Johnson, 15, and special projects organiser Maggie Gains from the Environmental Health do their share of sorting.

A few extra inches makes all the difference.

If you answer yes to the question ... "Do I need more space in my small family hatchback?" You should sit in, and stretch out in this.

The new Citroën Visa. For a small car, inside it's unusually big.

Rather like it's list of standard equipment; Front disc brakes, reversing lights, internally adjustable headlights, a clock, a washer/wiper at the back, cloth upholstery, twin speakers and aerial, plus of course, a big fifth door.

Now step out and peer under the bonnet. In the 49mpg* Visa Club (£3,112) you'll see a flat twin engine kept perfectly in tune by its revolutionary electronic ignition system, which never needs adjustment.

In the even better equipped Visa Super (£3,428) there's an overhead cam 1124cc job. Nippier, but still ridiculously economical, giving you 45mpg.*

Both these cars have front wheel drive and extra large luggage space.

And both have the Press saying what a lovely ride they are.

So duck not, strain not, and hunch not your back. Instead visit your local Citroën dealer and try out the car with the difference in inches.

You'll feel like a new man.

The new Citroën Visa. 5 door hatchback.

BRADFORD Jack Andrews (Cars) Ltd., Whetley Hill, Bradford. Tel: Bradford 495543 (Sales) Tel: Bradford 76285 (Service)
BROUGH Hessle Auto Engineers Ltd., Cross Roads, Elloughton, Nr. Brough. Tel: Hull 667225
CHESTERFIELD Gordon Lamb Holdings Ltd., Sheffield Road, Whittington Moor, Chesterfield. Tel: Chesterfield 451611
CLEETHORPES Lumley's Garage, 76-80 Brereton Avenue, Cleethorpes. Tel: Grimsby [illegible]
DONCASTER J. G. Allison (Continental) Ltd., Wheatley Hall Road, Doncaster. Tel: Doncaster [illegible]
GOLDTHORPE Dearneside Motor Co. Ltd., 106 Barnsley Road, Goldthorpe, Nr. Rotherham. Tel: Rotherham [illegible]
HALIFAX Mayfield Garage (Halifax) Ltd., Queens Road, Halifax. Tel: Halifax [illegible]
HARROGATE Croft & Blackburn Ltd., Leeds Road, Pannal, Harrogate. Tel: Harrogate [illegible]
HUDDERSFIELD Star Lane Motors Ltd., Star Lane, Milnsbridge, Huddersfield. Tel: Huddersfield 656164
HULL The Mytton Garage (Hull) Co. Ltd., 204a Anlaby Road, Hull. Tel: Hull 25849
LEEDS Bristol Street Motors (Leeds) Ltd., Water Lane, Leeds. Tel: Leeds 38091
LINCOLN Lindum Cars Ltd., 300 Wragby Road, Lincoln. Tel: Lincoln 31195-6 Tel: Lincoln 25407 (Parts)
MIRFIELD Calder Garage Ltd., 117 Huddersfield Road, Mirfield. Tel: Mirfield 493386
NORTHALLERTON Kellett & Pick Ltd., Alverton Garage, Romanby Road, Northallerton. Tel: Northallerton [illegible]
ROTHERHAM Freeway Cars Ltd., Bawtry Road, Hellaby, Maltby, Nr. Rotherham. Tel: Wickersley 3188
SCARBOROUGH Appletons Associates (Scarborough) Ltd., Main Street, Seamer, Scarborough [illegible]
SCUNTHORPE Baden Powell & Sons Ltd., 136-144 Ashby High Street, Scunthorpe. Tel: Scunthorpe [illegible] (Parts & Service)
SHEFFIELD [illegible] Cars Ltd., Northfield Road, Crookes, Sheffield. Tel: Sheffield 662441 & [illegible]
SKIPTON Angus (Skipton) Ltd., Otley Road, Skipton. Tel: Skipton 2282 & 2412
WAKEFIELD Comberhill (Yorkshire) Garages Ltd., Ings Road, Wakefield. Tel: Wakefield [illegible]
YORK Haw's Garage Ltd., Lowther Street, York. Tel: York 30710 & 22064

CITROËN Visa

*CITROËN VISA CLUB URBAN CYCLE 36.7MPG (7.7L/100KM), CONSTANT 56MPH (90KM/H) 48.7MPG (5.8L/100KM). CITROËN VISA SUPER URBAN CYCLE 33.6MPG (8.4L/100KM) CONSTANT 56MPH (90KM/H) 45.6MPG (6.2L/100KM) CONSTANT 75MPH (120KM/H) 33.6MPG (8.4L/100KM) PRICES INCLUDE CAR TAX, VAT AND INERTIA REEL SEAT BELTS, BUT EXCLUDE DELIVERY CHARGES [illegible] (INC VAT) AND NUMBER PLATES. PRICES CORRECT AT TIME OF GOING TO PRESS.

WELCOME TO THE
BIG FUR SALE
AT
NORTHERN
EXPORT
FURS
BIG GENUINE
REDUCTIONS
MINK Jkts. from £495
Coats from £995
FOX from £395
YOUR OLD FURS TAKEN IN PART EXCHANGE
Extra Special
Offers in
SQUIRREL ● MUSQUASH ● KID
● RACCOON ●
PERSIAN & MINK
PAW ● Etc. Etc.
FUN-FURS
TO CLEAR
from £29.50
ACCESS &
BARCLAYCARD-
Deferred terms available
Illustrated
PASTEL
MINK
£1,395
NORTHERN
EXPORT
FURS LTD
FISH STREET,
KIRKGATE, LEEDS 1
TEL: 30094

SUEDE & SHEEPSKIN
STOCK CLEARANCE
FROM ONE
OF THE
LONGEST
ESTABLISHED
SKIN SHOPS
IN THE
COUNTRY.
COMPARE
OUR
VALUES.
UNBEATABLE
PRICES
A small deposit reserves any garment.
MENS AND WOMENS
SHEEPSKINS
Model Coats Were £265 NOW £225
¾ Coats Were £120 NOW £79
Model Jackets Were £189 Now £149
LEATHER &
SUEDE
COATS & JACKETS
ALL REDUCED
FUN-FURS
JKTS FROM £29.50
COATS FROM £69.95
ACCESS & BARCLAYCARD WELCOME
Suede & Sheepskin Shop
7, KING EDWARD STREET
LEEDS
5, JAMES STREET
HARROGATE.

Dolomite —
Luxury and style with economy
Unrivalled for its stunning combination of performance and economy. The Dolomite offers luxurious comfort in a compact but roomy saloon with a choice of engine sizes
Choose your Dolomite now!
1979 T DOLOMITE SPRINT, 9,000 miles £4,595
1978 T DOLOMITE 1850 HL, 15,000 miles £3,595
1978 T DOLOMITE 1500 HL AUTO., 16,000 miles £3,550
1978 T DOLOMITE 1850 HL, 18,000 miles £3,550
1978 S DOLOMITE 1500, 14,000 miles £2,695
1978 S DOLOMITE 1500 HL, 14,000 miles £2,895
1977 S DOLOMITE 1500, 31,000 miles £2,495
1977 R DOLOMITE SPRINT, 12,000 miles £3,295
1977 R DOLOMITE 1500 HL, 25,000 miles £2,595
1976 P TRIUMPH 1500 TC AUTO., 20,000 miles .. £2,150
All these cars are covered by the outstanding Gauntlet Supreme Guarantee
ARNOLD G
WILSON
ARNOLD G. WILSON (LEEDS) LTD.
REGENT STREET, LEEDS 2. Telephone 30201

Halton, Leeds, 30 August 1980. Members and officials of the Boy's Brigade Fifth Leeds Company at work during their clean up operation in Primrose Lane, Halton. Six-year-old Ian Morley, of Baronsway, Whitkirk, is in the foreground.

Former Leeds United and England manager Don Revie is pictured escorting daughter Kim to the Yorkshire Television Studios, Kirkstall Road, Leeds, where she was interviewed about her recently released first pop record, *It's Come Back Again.*

Leeds Theatres, Grand Theatre, 24 November 1980. When the Grand Theatre opened its door to the public on their 'Grand Open Day' a queue formed as people waited eagerly for an insight into the workings of the theatre. Jeff Riley, 21, an electrician is showing the new computer display deck, which controls stage and house lighting, to Mrs Kath Wardle and her daughter Chrissie, six, of Greenhill Gardens, Wortley, Leeds.

Caribbean Carnival, Leeds, 25 August 1980.

Calverley, Leeds, 18 September 1980. Mrs Judith Murray (left), secretary of the Calverley Residents Action Group, and Mrs Margaret Angus count the traffic.

marr LTD
OVENS
DRYERS
WASHERS
LEEDS
GHO 584W

RAF Apprentice

It's the best technical training there is. Full time, fully paid. And in just three years you're a fully qualified engineering technician.

But first you need to be 16-18½, with four 'O' levels grade C or above, including Maths and a Science subject (or equivalent).

And you need to know more. So ask us more.

Drop in for a chat at:

10, Bond Court, Leeds 432914

26, Kirkgate, Bradford 721797

33, Westgate, Huddersfield 25345

ENGINEERING TECHNICIAN

WHERE CAN YOU FIND A CLEANER, CHEAPER WAY OF PACKAGING?

Investigate the benefits of the **THERMOGRIP** system from Bostik.

It is a simple, versatile, efficient and proven system of glue guns and hot melt glue sticks which provide unrivalled performance.

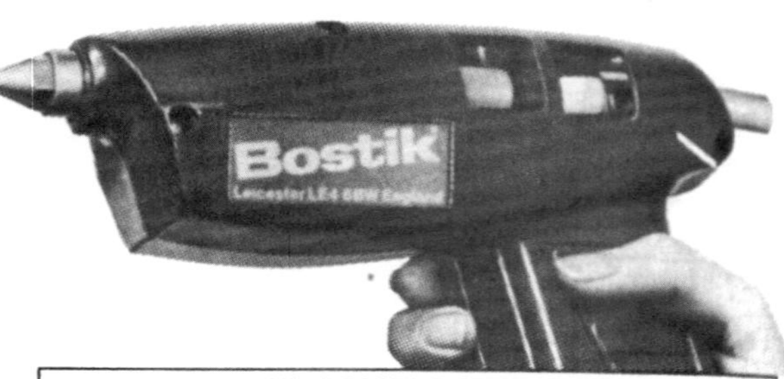

- Bonds and seals
- Assembles
- Reclaims and repairs
- Saves drying time
- Speeds up gluing methods
- Avoids pack damage
- Uses lower cost pack formats
- Uses lower cost board
- Reclaims reject packs
- Bonds most material
- Anyone can use it (13 amp socket)
- FDA approved
- Low capital cost – pays for itself in days

See one in action, without obligation – contact your Bostik distributor.

YOUR BOSTIK DISTRIBUTOR

Mr. Leigh, Sidney Beaumont, Sydenham Road, Domestic Street Industrial Estate, Leeds.
Tel: 0532 458729.

Bostik
EMHART

BOSTIK THERMOGRIP 295 GLUE GUN PACKAGING PROGRAMME FOR BUSINESS

VALLANCES

12 MONTHS INTEREST FREE CREDIT†

OFFER ENDS SAT., 12th SEPT.

ON A WIDE RANGE OF PRODUCTS
HERE ARE JUST A FEW EXAMPLES:

£249.99

ITT CT3307 20" COLOUR TV
8 programme, push button tuner, compact monitor styling and comes complete with matching video stand.

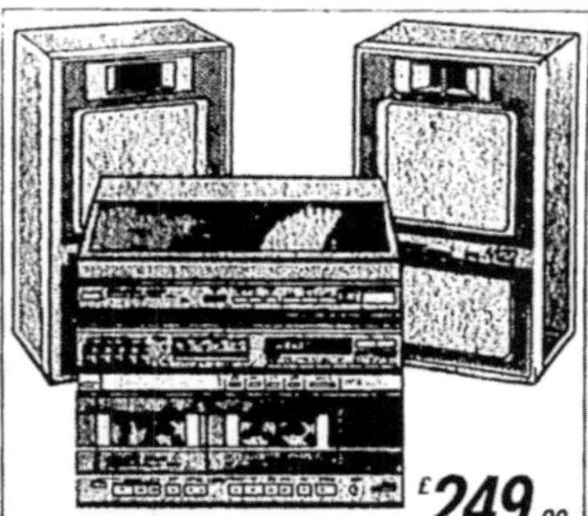

£249.99

FISHER M22 MIDI HIFI SYSTEM
Twin cassette with Dolby 'B' noise reduction, 5 band graphic equaliser, 25 watts RMS per channel, soft touch controls, belt drive turntable with linear tracking.

SAVE £50

£299.99

TOSHIBA ER7900 MICROWAVE
10 Power Levels up to 650 watts output. 0.95 cu.ft. capacity. Choice of 25 pre-set menus takes the guessing out of timing. Heat and hold facility to keep food just right after cooking. Turntable and auto-defrost. Was £349.99.

REMOTE CONTROL

SAVE £20

£399.99

HITACHI CPT2278 COLOUR TV
22" Teletext colour TV with full infra red remote control. 19 channel tuner with LED display. Headphone socket and RGB input. Complete with matching TV/Video stand. Was £419.99.

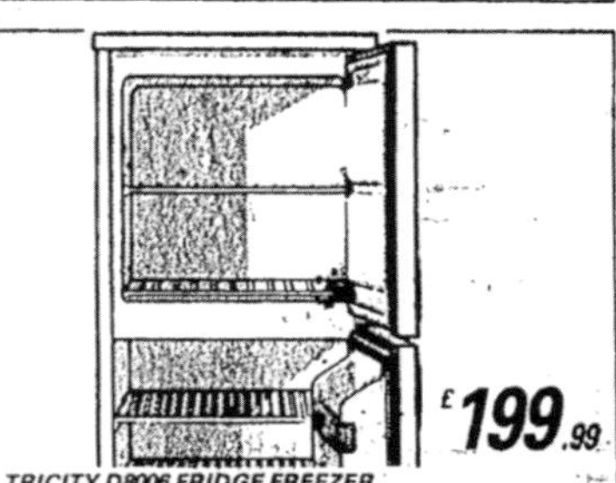

£199.99

TRICITY D8006 FRIDGE FREEZER
This slim-line model (under 20" wide) is ideal for the smaller kitchen. 2.9 cu.ft. Freezer with shelves on 6.00 cu.ft. auto defrost fridge with full width salad crisper and adjustable door storage.

£269.99

HOOVER A3572 AUTOMATIC WASHING MACHINE
A versatile automatic washing machine with variable spin speeds of 800 RPM. Full 10lb wash load with half load facility. Finished in Beige and White.

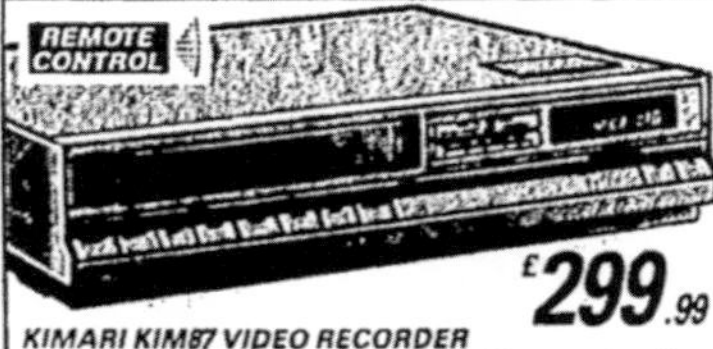

REMOTE CONTROL

£299.99

KIMARI KIM87 VIDEO RECORDER
Japanese front loading, slim line, VHS video recorder with 14 day 4 event timer. HQ facility with picture search forward and back. Full infra red remote control hand set.

£299.99

HOTPOINT 8633A FRIDGE FREEZER
3.5 cu.ft. auto defrost fridge with reversible door on 4.2 cu.ft. freezer which stores 70lb of frozen food, has removable baskets with transparent fronts to keep in the cold.

FREE WALKMAN

£249.99

SONY COM19 MIDI HIFI SYSTEM
A midi hifi system with twin cassette deck with high speed dubbing. 5 band graphic equaliser and 3 band manual analogue tuner. Output is 20 watts RMS

SAVE £20

£399.99

HOTPOINT 9901 WASHER/DRYER
This deluxe model is Britain's best selling Washer/dryer. It's a condenser model which means no vent kit is necessary. The 1000 RPM spin speed ensures a very dry finish. Available in Almond, White or Polar White. Was £419.99

CREDIT EXAMPLE:	
Tricity D8006 Fridge Freezer	£199.99
Deposit – 10%	£19.99
Balance	£180.00
12 payments of:	£15.00
APR	NIL

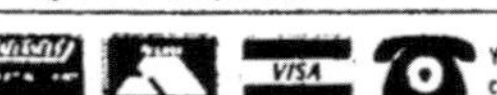

You can telephone your order to our store quoting your credit card number or using our C.O.D. facility pay the deliveryman

Products subject to availability. Prices correct at time of going to press. Offers made for a limited period only. Reduced price items may not have been offered at the higher price for 28 consecutive days in the last six months but have been sold at it in our Headrow Leeds branch. †Subject to status. Written quotations available on request. APR 0%. Licensed credit broker.

20 NEW MARKET STREET, LEEDS TEL: 436831
THE HEADROW, LEEDS TEL: 433213
44 DAISY HILL, DEWSBURY TEL: 462352
ALSO AT WAKEFIELD, HARROGATE
AND THROUGHOUT THE REGION.

BEST FOR CHOICE · BEST FOR PRICE · BEST FOR SERVICE

Leeds, 25 November 1980. Happy greeting for Henry Cooper, on a visit to Howson-Algraphy, Leeds, from Caroline Somes (left), publicity manager, and Rosemary Jones, PRO. The firm sponsored Wetherby Lions' boxing night at the Old Swan, Harrogate, and Henry presented the prizes. Proceeds were for a gym at Boston Spa Youth Centre, and camps in India.

Leeds, 25 November 1980. Radio PBS Leeds Infirmary's Hospital Broadcasting Service is back on the air after an eight month silence. Programme presenters, left to right: Paul Cargill, Steve Hirst, Trevor Griffiths, Martin Croft and Alan Dee.

Chapeltown, 16 December 1980. Angry pickets demonstrating against a new Leeds 'sex shop'.

Leeds, Beeston, 1980s. Junction of Lodge Lane and Beeston Road.

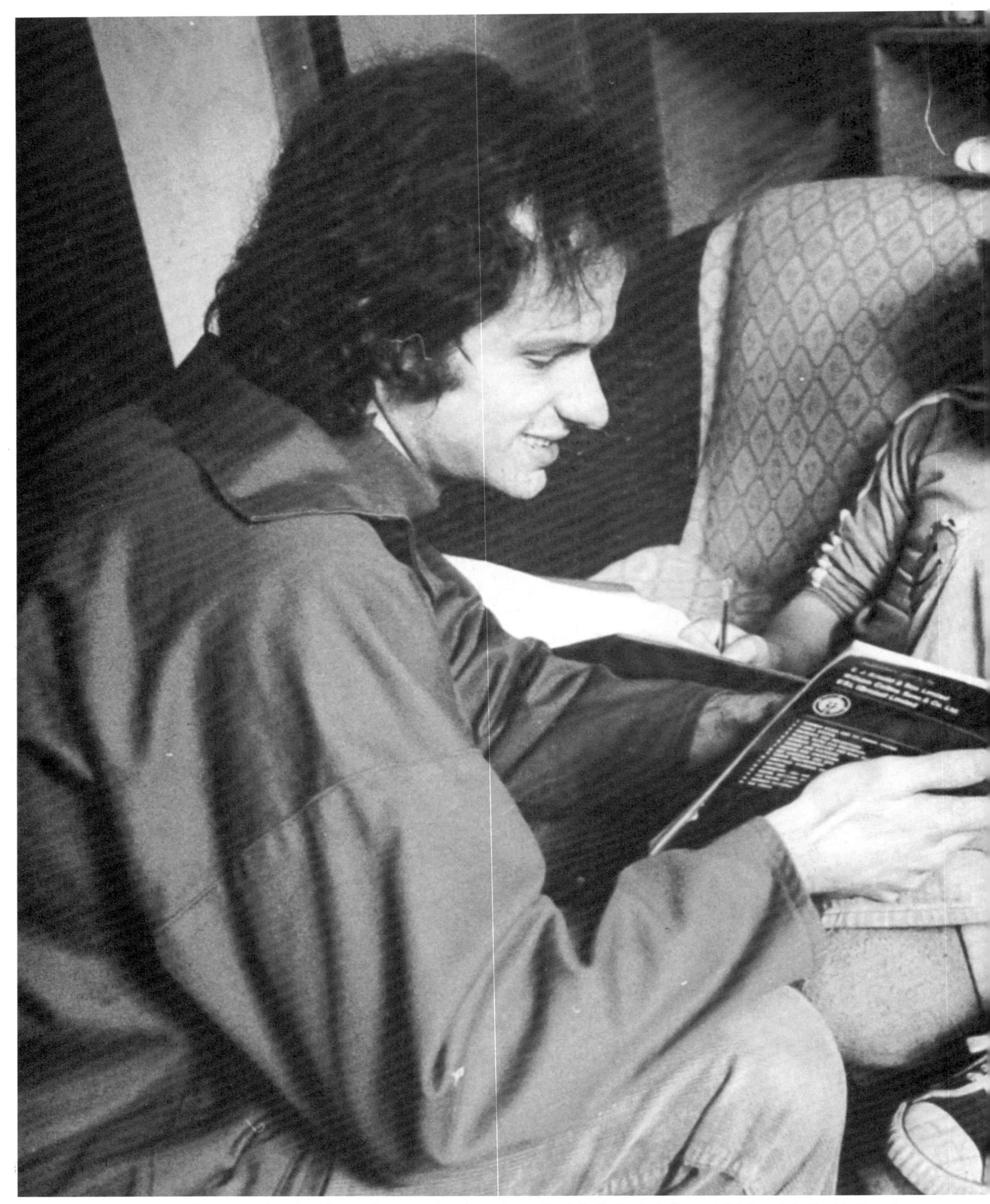

Class in session at Leeds Free School with teacher, Ian Paul and pupils, Mark (15), left, and Richard (12), 12 October 1980.

"it's got to be the film of the year – and deservedly."
SUNDAY PEOPLE
"MASTERPIECE FOR BURTON..."
John Du Pre, SUNDAY PEOPLE
"HURT surely deserves an Oscar."
John Blake, THE SUN
GEORGE ORWELL'S TERRIFYING VISION COMES TO THE SCREEN.
1984
15
JOHN HURT · RICHARD BURTON
in Michael Radford's film of George Orwell's NINETEEN EIGHTY-FOUR
with SUZANNA HAMILTON · CYRIL CUSACK
A Virgin Films/Umbrella-Rosenblum Films production
Executive Producer MARVIN J. ROSENBLUM · Co-producers AL CLARK & ROBERT DEVEREUX
Produced by SIMON PERRY · Written & Directed by MICHAEL RADFORD
Virgin
A VIRGIN FILM RELEASE in association with TWENTIETH CENTURY FOX
through U.K. FILM DISTRIBUTORS LTD
STARTS TODAY ODEON LEEDS
3.05, 5.35, 8.15

SELF-EMPLOYED & BUSINESS PEOPLE
CONTRACT HIRE & LEASING
'D' REG SUNNY 1.3LX
£31.86 PER WK
WE CAN SUPPLY ONE CAR OR ONE HUNDRED CARS!
'E' REG CABSTAR
£38.68 PER WK
CASH BACK FOR YOUR PRESENT CAR
'D' BLUEBIRD TURBO 2X £46.65
'D' MICRA 1.0L £20.76
'D' FIESTA 1.1L £21.74
'D' METRO CITY £20.49
'D' ORION 1.6L £31.40
'D' ROVER 216SE £40.56
'D' SIERRA 1.6L £32.97
'D' ESCORT 1.3L £29.35
'D' SIERRA 1.8L £33.89
'D' CAVALIER 1.6 £35.24
'D' GOLF C 1.3 £33.84
'E' URVAN £39.97
'E' 1 TON PICKUP £32.06
'E' VANETTE £35.02
'E' SUNNY VAN £28.30
IMPROVE YOUR CASH FLOW
8PM WEEKDAYS & 5.30 SAT & SUN
D.C.COOK
MAIN DEALER SUPERCENTRES
BARNSLEY
(0226) 206657
BRADFORD
(0274) 729999

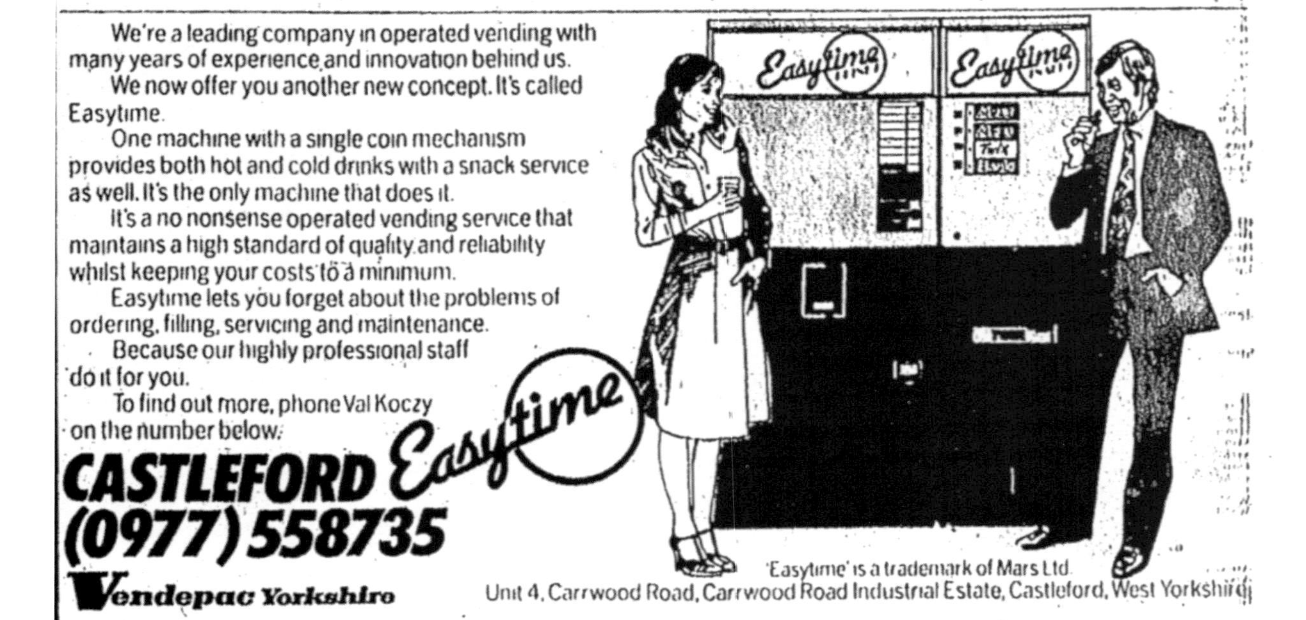
ONE MACHINE.
TWO REFRESHMENT SERVICES.
We're a leading company in operated vending with many years of experience and innovation behind us.
We now offer you another new concept. It's called Easytime.
One machine with a single coin mechanism provides both hot and cold drinks with a snack service as well. It's the only machine that does it.
It's a no nonsense operated vending service that maintains a high standard of quality and reliability whilst keeping your costs to a minimum.
Easytime lets you forget about the problems of ordering, filling, servicing and maintenance.
Because our highly professional staff do it for you.
To find out more, phone Val Koczy on the number below.
CASTLEFORD
(0977) 558735
Easytime
Vendepac Yorkshire
'Easytime' is a trademark of Mars Ltd.
Unit 4, Carrwood Road, Carrwood Road Industrial Estate, Castleford, West Yorkshire

Cross Gates, Leeds, 1981. The pedestrian crossing at Station Road which is being replaced with a pelican crossing.

Leeds, 10 March 1981. The scrapyard near the junction of Bath Road and Water Lane at Holbeck, Leeds.

Leeds, 26 March 1981. A piece of the past has been planted in the grounds of brand new Castleton Primary School, Armley, Leeds. For the staff and pupils of Castleton, dubbed 'The school for scandal' when it was in its Victorian Armley Road premises, now have the 100-year-old castle-shaped gatepost top as a keepsake. Pictured are Sarah Trigg, five, and Mr John Creswell, of Witt, Newton and Co., stonemasons, installing the old stone on its new site, watched by staff and pupils.

30 March 1981. Bomb disposal robot in Leeds.

12 June 1981. Writer James Herriot at Austicks bookshop on the Headrow, Leeds, autographing his latest book.

Cottage Road Cinema 1982. Mr Osman Pickthall (right) outside Cottage Road Cinema, Headingley, with manager Mr Derek Todd.

29 January 1982. Keverne, a 6ft blue wooden sculpture and the latest aquisition of Leeds Polytechnic foyer. He is the work of former polytechnic fine arts student, Mike Winstone.

Leeds, 12 June 1981. The City of Leeds College of Music Symphony Orchestra are giving a concert of popular music at Leeds Town Hall tonight. Soloists at rehearsal are, from left: Paul Gardham, 18, of West Park, Leeds, Janice Close, 19, singer from Sheffield, Rosemary Hay, 18, of Bramhope, Leeds, singer, Neil Atkinson, 23, of Sunderland, clarinet, Sarah Lyle, 18, of Lawnswood.

Leeds, 13 October 1981. A traffic warden studies one of the new parking meters in Park Square.

Leeds, 18 November 1981. Although he enjoys playing football as a hobby, 10-year-old Christopher Bennett's real skill is on a chess board. A pupil at Manston Middle School, Christopher, of Kelmscott Green, Cross Gates, has been playing chess since the age of four and has just added the title of Leeds School's under-12 champion to his list of successes.

Leeds City Station, 10 December 1981. The four Leeds councillors who drive high speed trains, from left, Bryan North, Walter Thurlow, Frank Stringer and Mick Lyons.

Mr Peter Judge, outside his home (right) in Hoxton Grove, Leeds, while demolition work goes ahead, 10 August 1981.

25 September 1981, Horsforth Golf Club. Cessna 152 which overshot the runway at Leeds Bradford Airport. The pilot, Mr Norman Hudson, 51, insurance broker, of Southway, Tranmere Park, Guiseley, Leeds, was unhurt.

7 January 1982. Great George Street and Cookridge Street, Leeds.

WATSON
LTD.

Leeds, 3 February 1982. Allerton Grange High School's head boy Ivor Rowlands with a bottle of milk. Pupils at Allerton Grange High School, Talbot Avenue, Leeds, led by Ivor Rowlands, claim Leeds City Council is not showing a lot of bottle by making 60 per cent profit on the third of a pint of milk on sale in the School's cash cafeteria. 'The council buy the milk from Associated Dairies for 6 and a quarter pence and we have to pay 10p for it', said Ivor, 17.

26 May 1982. The five members of the Shape Up North community arts group with their mural in Little London Community Centre, Leeds: from left, Ruth Keep, 26, Robert Greenwood, 25, Chris Humphrey, 24, David Collins, 20, and Susan Billings, 23.

Leeds, Eastgate 23 April 1982. Herbert Brown and Son Ltd.

The musical youngsters of the 14th East Leeds Scouts and Guides Marching Band, are rapidly making a name for themselves. They have been playing regularly at different events since the band was formed 18 months ago, and are expecting more engagements this summer. The band, led by Mr David Jones, has brass, woodwind and drums. Mr Jones, an experienced brass band player, who formed the East Leeds band, said: 'What we could do with is some help from an ex-brass bander who could help with the pracitces.' Leeds, April 1982

Lassie, a four-year-old black and tan mongrel, is hardly ever likely to get dog tired. For the simple reason that when she goes out and about she travels in style – in the open cockpit of a scooter combination. Lassie's introduction to three-wheel travel began when Mrs Sue Cairns, of Tithe Barn Lane, Bardsey, took delivery of a Vespa combo. Says Mrs Cairns, whose husband Jim is a Leeds motorcycle dealer: 'She goes almost everywhere with me. She loves it and is no trouble at all even when I leave the scooter and Lassie parked at the road side to do my shopping.' Soon, Lassie, who was acquired from the Canine Rescue Service after being ill-treated and neglected will notch up 1,000 miles. She will ride north in style when Sue, Jim and their two children, Paul, 13, and Chrstine, 12, leave on a scooter and motorbike tour of Scotland. Leeds, 17 June 1982.

Bramley, 4 September 1982. Vintage 1953 fire engine, one of five specially built for Leeds City Fire Service in September 1953, is travelling around Britain on a 1,400-mile charity fund raising marathon in aid of the British Heart Foundation and Fire Services National Benevolent Fund. And it paused for a quick stop over in Leeds, where it served at Bramley Fire Station until 1970. Pictured with the engine are Dartford fireman Sub Officer Peter New (in cab), top, Fireman David Copper (left) and Fireman John Meakins, watched by three members of Leeds Fire Station (from left) ADO David Abbott, Sub Officer Gary Holmes and Leading Fireman Pete Bramham.

22 September 1982. Leeds, Mill Hill. Bibis Restaurant.

Leeds, 30 September 1982. Railmen in Leeds who keep the Inter City 125 High Speed trains running have received framed congratulatory scrolls for their part in the trains covering an amazing 25 million miles in just four years. Mr Paterson, right, presents the scrolls to, left to right: Mr Eric Moore of Bradford, Holbeck depot, Mr Harry Cowling of

Whinmoor, Leeds, Neville Hill Depot, Mr John Fletcher of Burmantofts, Leeds, Neville Hill and Mr George Hodgson of Halton Moor, Leeds, Neville Hill. The four represented all BR staff connected with the 125 trains.

Three hundred people braved the cold today to welcome Leeds City Station's latest distinguished visitor. Yorkshire based Class Forty Preservation Society has raised enough money to secure spare parts and a future, for one diesel. Tim Knight puts a Christmas cracker sign on the front of the engine before the start of the journey to Dundee today, 18 December 1982.

From the traffic island near the International Pool in Leeds, Frank Howarth holds aloft his sign asking for work – in the hope that some passing driver can solve his dilemma, 3 November 1982.

Leeds, Harehills, 4 December 1982. Sixty years of scouting at St Cyprian's Church, Coldcotes Avenue. Left to right: Christopher Brown (10), Ian Short (9), Mark Keeler (8), Robert Field (12) and Martin Wallis (12). The boys of the 8th North Vale group.

18 June 1982. Leeds Bradford Airport. The wreckage of an old aircraft is set ablaze to simulate fire-fighting conditions.

Leeds, 7 January 1983. Corpus Christi School. Tony Raferty (left), 13, and Andrew Walton work on an electronic 'car' at the new technology course at Corpus Christi School.

Leeds, 25 January 1983. The Windmill Hotel, at Seacroft.

2 February 1983. The storms brought an unexpected bonanza to shoppers in Leeds Market. More that 800 customers got the bargain of a lifetime when butcher Trevor Middleton, thinking his shops might be closed because of the damage to Leeds market, cut his proceeds 'To the Bone' and gave away vegetables with the meat. Mr Trevor Middleton (right) of Middleton Hargreaves butchers, with some of his staff who helped sell the meat, from left, Carl Hilton, Brian Longbottom, Christopher Farmer, Roy Marsden, Colin Clark, Jackie Morgan and Graham Wray.

Leeds, 11 January 1983. Cross Green Industrial Estate, Babington Car Spares. Leon Parish, left, and John Eastwood with their DIY crusher.

Leeds, Austicks Bookshop, 16 February 1983. Spike Milligan with Gaby Proctor, 16, (left) and Helen Brown, 17, of Leeds.

Leeds, 8 November 1983. Leeds Maternity Hospital.

Leeds, 31 January 1983. Concourse House, Wellington Street. Factory and warehouse fires.

Leeds, 18 May 1983. Equipping 334 polling stations in Leeds with ballot boxes and election notices has been a long job for Leeds Electoral registration office clerk messengers Wilf Lister (left) and Peter Sharpe. The pair have spent most of the time leading up to polling day in the Belgrave House storage room, getting the boxes ready to serve the city's eight constituencies. About 50 of the boxes have needed repairing after suffering damage at the May local council elections, but this is put down to wear and tear. 'The most common problem with the boxes has been damaged locks, but some of them have seen many years of election service', said Mr Tom McCarthy, deputy elections officer. Each box is equipped with notices, stamping equipment, and pencils. 'More than 600,000 ballot papers were handed out to presiding officers when they were sworn in on Tuesday to give their declaration of secrecy', said Mr McCarthy.

Leeds, 12 September 1983. The clock at Leeds University shows that it is after 4pm. And at that time until 6.30pm, a new bus lane is now in operation between Portland Crescent and Blackman Lane. Accordingly cars should move over to give priority to bus traffic in that nearside Lane, but some motorists still drive through.

Leeds, Middleton, 3 July 1983. Six-year-old Natalie Booth, of St Helen's Gardens, Adel, Leeds, meets a trainee locomotive fireman, Mr Paul Whiteley, during a transport rally. Steam fans were pushed and pulled along the Middleton Light Railway to demonstrate its potential as a tourist attraction.

Leeds, Headingley, 18 October 1983. Fred Trueman arrives for a meeting concerning the sacking of Geoffrey Boycott.

Leeds, Pudsey, 19 October 1983. Opera North's orchestra, the English Northern Philharmonia, celebrated its fifth birthday yesterday. The principal conductor and artistic director of Opera North, Mr David Lloyd-Jones, cut the cake at Pudsey Civic Hall watched by the orchestra manager Mr Ian Killik; the chorus master, Mr John Pryce-Jones, holding the cake, and the leader of the orchestra, Mr David Greed, right.

Leeds, 28 November 1983. Actor Anthony Perkins arriving at Leeds City Station.

Leeds, 30 November 1983. Mr Robert Maxwell addresses members of the National Graphical Association during his visit to Leeds yesterday to open Petty's new plant. Printing magnate Mr Robert Maxwell today launched a scathing attack on government industrial relations legislation while visiting a Leeds printing works. Mr Maxwell flew into Leeds by helicopter to open a new press at Petty & Sons, Whitehall Road, Leeds.

1 December 1983. Leeds United manager Eddie Gray ready for the big lights switch on with the Lord Mayor of Leeds, Councillor Martin Dodgson.

Leeds, Elland Road, 30 December 1983. It was change over time at Elland Road today when Leeds United chairman Manny Cussins handed over the reins to Leslie Silver. Leslie Silver, the club's vice-chairman for the past two years officially succeeded Mr Manny Cussins as chairman.

Merrion Centre, Leeds 1984. Interior of the Merrion Centre.

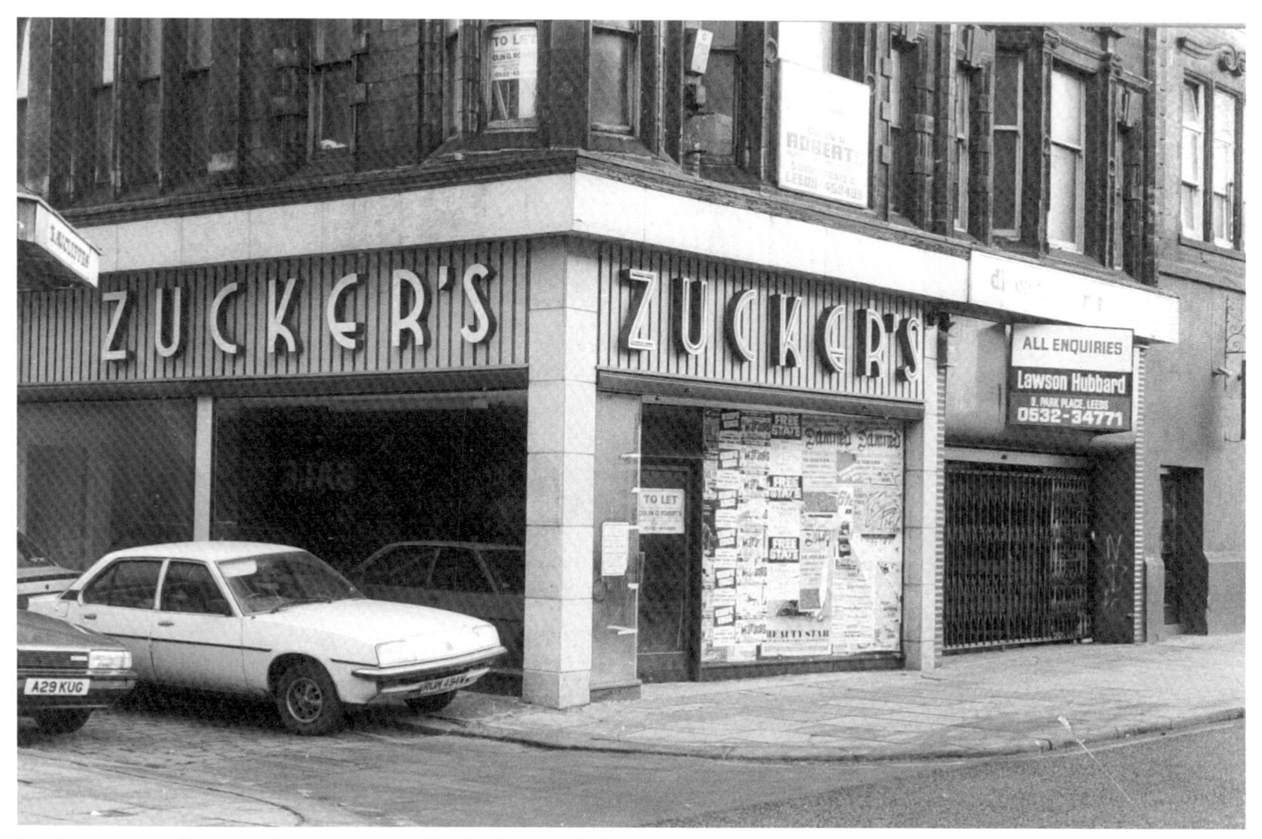

Leeds, Duncan Street, 6 January 1984. Zucker's closed shop.

Leeds, 5 April 1984. Park Lane. Leeds City Council was today granted a possession order for the former Rates Office in Leeds City centre, occupied earlier this week by a group of 'squatters'. The squatters's supporters are festooned in

the old rates office in Park Lane with paper as a protest against and eviction ruling.

Road Sweepers, 30 January 1984. Stanley road cleansing department, Leeds, Lynn Smith.

Leeds, Eastgate 23 February 1984. Mr Louis Karim, pictured against the bus shelter, which he claims was blocking his coffee bar.

Leeds, Moortown, 12 April 1984. Comic actor Roy Kinnear turned to *The Twits* when he visited Allerton Grange Middle School, Moortown, Leeds. The television and stage star, who is appearing this week at the Grand Theatre, Leeds, took time off for a spot of story telling in the school hall and is pictured here with some of the second-year pupils.

Leeds, 8 June 1984. John Ramsden with a 3ft 8in long salmon, possibly the biggest ever to land at Leeds Fish market. The fish, caught in the North Sea off the Tyne, was worth nearly £120 when cut into steaks.

5 June 1984. Former World light heavyweight champion John Conteh will be hoping to knock out a few critics when he appears in Leeds next week. Conteh, 33, is appearing in a major role in Willy Russell's hit musical *Blood Brothers* which opens at the Leeds Grand Theatre on 12 June as part of a 10-week national tour.

Leeds, 17 June 1984. Some of the best buskers in the city brought music to the ears of shoppers and passers-by in Leeds at the weekend, as they took part in a 'play-off' to decide who will perform at the Lord Mayor's Charity Gala Concert next weekend. Eight talented street acts gathered at the Garden of Rest, outside Leeds Central Library to entertain the crowds who were enjoying a sunny afternoon. First on the bill was a busker who has been further than most to pursue his 'art'. L.R. Airey , of Otley Road, Leeds, who performs under the name of Leo, is a singer/guitarist who has toured the Shetlands plus folk clubs in the Falklands, as well as Antarctic bases. Each busker was given 10 minutes to impress the judges in the competition, organised by Leeds Leisure Services in association with the *Yorkshire Evening Post.* Without any instrumental assistance 84-year-old Franke Hall, of Lidgett Towers, Leeds, sang a collection of old songs with just a walking stick and trilby hat as his only props – a performance which attracted frinedly cheers from the crowd gathered to watch. Also singing unaccompanied was Danny Freeman, of Oakwood Avenue, Leeds, who gave a rousing rendition of *Edelwiess* to please the spectators. Often seen at pubs and clubs in the Leeds area, Ken Eagleton, of Carrholm Drive, Chapel-Allerton. Pictured – the Two Buskateers, Robert Hunt and Neil Clay, in action.

Leeds, Roundhay Park, 11 August 1984. Anglers Henry Pollard (66), left, and oldest competitor Ezra Naylor (79) walk to their pegs at Roundhay Park Lake, Leeds, before taking part in the senior citizens angling match.

7 November 1984, Elsworth Street, Armley, Leeds. Inside the squatters home in Elsworth Street, Armley, Wendy Thorne feeds her baby Ben (eight weeks) while her other child Charlie (18 months) sleeps.

Leeds, City Square, 16 November 1984. Ronald Magill, alias Amos Brearley in Leeds to mark the launch of Help the Aged's Northern Christmas Appeal. Throwing the fake snowballs were (from left) Parminder Binji, Matthew Birch, Stuart Perkins and Erica Withington, all 13.

Leeds, Beeston, 30 January 1985. Trentham Street sub post office.

Leeds Cinemas. The Tower Picture House on 5 March 1985. Tom Mellor, 83, who was the projectionist at the Tower when it opened in 1920, will witness its closure when the curtain falls tomorrow. He made a special request to the cinema's manager, Mrs Joyce Stocks (pictured with Mr Mellor) to be there at the end.

Leeds, Duncan Sreet, 7 March 1985. Call Lane and Duncan Street.

Leeds, 23 April 1985. Geoff Thompson in the projection room at the Hyde Park Picture House, Leeds: 'Cinema is in

Leeds, 7 March 1985. The Wellesley Hotel, Wellington Street.

HOTEL
HOTEL ENTRANCE
FOOD

Leeds Bradford Airport, 28 May 1985. British Airtours TriStar airliner with 416 people on board plunged off the end of the runway yesterday. Some of the sightseers who flocked to Scotland Lane, Horsforth, today, to see the crashed TriStar.

Leeds 7 July 1985. Bruce Springsteen concert in Roundhay Park.

umbro
REFEREE
F.I.F.A.

Leeds, 28 July 1985. England v West Germany. Replay of the 1966 World Cup Final at Elland Road. Exchange of pennants at Elland Road for the England and West German captains, Bobby Moore and Uwe Seller prior to kick-off with referee Mr J.K. Taylor (centre).

Leeds, 11 September 1985. Rose Forgrove Chess Club, based in Seacroft, Leeds, which has 80 members, won through six regional qualifying matches before travelling down to the national final in July. And when the five-man team beat King's head by 3.5 points to 1.5 they became the first team outside London to win the minor section championship. Back from left: Steve Spencer, Benjamin Science, Dave Smith, Ian Smith, Luke Bond, Royston Bond. Sitting from left: Tony Pawson, Mark White, Simon Holdsworth, Stan Alexandrowicz.

Leeds, 26 September 1985. On the march…at front (from left), Mrs Joan Hilton, Ronnie Hilton, Mgr Michael Buckley, Harry Higgins, chairman of Leeds Outdoor Stallholders Group, and Eddie Cornell, chairman of Leeds Market Tenants and Traders Association, pictured with other angry stallholders.

Chapel Allerton, Leeds. 26 September 1985. Club manager Bill Lumsden on the indoor tennis complex.

Leeds, 12 November 1985. Leeds market trader Winston Cornell has narrowly avoided a legal battle with a top London department store over the name of his market stall – 'Arrods'. Mr Cornell named his hardware stall 'Arrods' as a joke when he set up in Kirkgate Open Market seven years ago, he was stunned to receive a letter from Harrod's London solicitors, threatening to start High Court proceedings unless he changes the name and the olive green and gold sign above his stall.

Leeds, 11 January 1986. Members of the West Yorkshire Passenger Transport Authority are kept waiting at Leeds City Station. British Rail's newest flag flier – the prestigious 'Sprinter' train – limped into Leeds station today on its Yorkshire debut, an embarrassing 22 minutes late. Red-faced BR officials and representatives of the new West Yorkshire Transport Authority pace up and down Platform No. 3 looking at their watches as the train failed to appear. It was due to take VIPS on a tour of the West Yorkshire rail network beginning at 9.30am, and publicity information proclaimed: 'The quicker way from here to there in West Yorkshire'.

Crossgates, Leeds, 7 April 1986. Crossgates station.

Leeds, Headingley, 1 May 1986. Geoffrey Boycott arrives at Headingley for the Second XI Championship match against Glamorgan.

Leeds, 20 June 1986. Mr Carl Waite, of Wakefield, and Miss Andrea Bailey, of Tingley, admire the mural at Leeds City Station.

Leeds, 6 August 1986. Mr Paul Jackson at his garage business in Assembly Street, near Leeds Market where he was attacked by a khaki and yellow Italian grass snake. It was taken away by Chief Inspector Sid Jenkins of the RSPCA. 'It made a dive for me. I jumped out of the way just in time,' said Mr Jackson.

Leeds, 26 August 1986. PC Billy Gilmore in step with Milli Harewood.

Leeds, 20 October 1986. Leeds market traders today delivered a petition signed by a quarter of a million people opposing council plans to redevelop their market – and they carried it in a coffin. Traders dressed as pallbearers delivering the petition in a coffin to Leeds City Council planning officials.

Leeds, 3 November 1986. Yorkshire cricketer Kevin Sharp was part of the Leeds Leisure Services cricket school to talk to a group of youngsters at Royal Park development programme at Middle School, Headingley.

It's the CARNELL
CASH BACK
ORDER YOUR CAR MIDWEEK AND YOU WILL GET
£100 OFF THE ADVERTISED PRICE
CASH IN HAND!
OPEN LATE WEDNESDAY TILL 10 p.m.
VAUXHALL CAVALIERS
NOW ONLY £6695
NOW ONLY £6895
NOW ONLY £7095
NOW ONLY £7295
NOW ONLY £7495
FREE VALETING
IMMEDIATE DELIVERY
'E' Registered
VAUXHALL ASTRAS
ONLY £24.47 per week
SAVE £927.84
IMMEDIATE DELIVERY
1.3L 3 door ONLY £26.38 per week SAVE £1094.60
1.3L 5 door ONLY £28.30 per week SAVE £1270.36
'E' Registered
VAUXHALL NOVA 1.2 CLUB
ONLY £21.23 per week
SAVE £996.00
IMMEDIATE DELIVERY
'E' Registered
CARNELL
LOW LANE HORSFORTH LEEDS
OPEN MON-FRI
OPEN ALL WEEKEND
HOTLINE

AUSTIN ROVER
Mini City
Bristol Street Motors
Special Offer £3347 on the road
SPECIFICATION INCLUDES:
Economical 1 litre engine
Constant 56 m.p.h. shows an economical 60.5 m.p.g.
12 inch steel wheels
Black wheel arch spats
6 year anti-corrosion warranty
Front disc brakes
Radial ply tyres
Heated rear window
Sawtooth cloth seats inserts
Plus Our Super Finance Deal
only £99 Deposit
PLUS 36 MONTHLY PAYMENTS OF £122.70
Total Credit Price £4,516.28
A.P.R. 23.3%
LICENSED CREDIT BROKERS
The right deal right now
FROM AUSTIN ROVER
Bristol Street Motors
Water Lane, Holbeck, Leeds 11.
Tel: 438091.

LONDON
£29 SAVER
RETURN
SAVER RETURNS
FROM LEEDS
2 hours 30 mins Approx. Journey Time
Hourly service Monday to Saturday
FOR RAIL INFORMATION RING:
(LEEDS) 448133
InterCity

UNBEATABLE PRICES – OR WE PAY!
YES, WE'LL REFUND THE DIFFERENCE
If you buy any product from Charlie Browns and find that you can buy the same product cheaper from another retail company in town within 7 days.
EXHAUSTS from £14.95
Ford Cortina MK 3/4/5 Ex GI Estate & 2 3 £24.95
Morris Ital 1700/2000 All models £42.95
Ford Escort Mk 1 2 1 1.3 Ex GT/RS Van Estate & Automatic £19.95
Vauxhall Cavalier 1600/1900 up to '81 (2 box system) Ex Sport Hatchback £32.95
Austin Metro Ex MG & Vanden Plas £35.95
Vauxhall Cavalier 1600/1900 1981 on £74.95
Mini Saloon Estate Single Box System £14.95
Vauxhall Chevette £31.95
Ford Escort Mk 3 1300 1600 Ex XR3 & Van £46.95
Ford Sierra 1.3 1.6 2.0 Complete system £54.95
Ford Fiesta 950 100 up to 1983 Ex XR2 & Low Compression £18.95
Ford Sierra 1.3 1.6 2.0 Ex Front Pipe £39.95
Morris Marina 1.3 1.8 Ex 1.7 & TC £19.95
Ford Capri Mk2 1.3 1.6 2.0 Ex GT £35.95
TYRES from £18.95
DUNLOP
145 SR13 SP Elite Steel Radial Car Tyre T/L £22.95
155 SR13 SP Elite Steel Radial Car Tyre T/L £23.95
165 SR13 SP Elite Steel Radial Car Tyre T/L £25.95
LEE
145 SR13 Steel Radial Car Tyre T/L £18.95
155 SR13 Steel Radial Car Tyre T/L £19.95
165 SR13 Steel Radial Car Tyre T/L £21.95
ALL PRICES INCLUDE VAT!
FREE ANTI-FREEZE CHECK
Premium Anti-Freeze 2 Litres £1.99
TERRIFIC VALUE!
WD-40 Maintenance Spray (200ml) £1.25
Also available (400ml) £2.49
Tungstone low maintenance batteries Full 2 year guarantee From only £14.95
Full range of Bosch spark plugs (non resistor type) From only £3.29 (pack of 4)
Ring Halogen Twinset Driving Lamps £7.99 per pair
25% EXTRA FREE
Power Winter Screenwash 2 litres PLUS 25% Extra Free £1.79
Contour Universal Fabric Car Mats (set of 4) £3.99
GREAT VALUE!
Charlie Browns 5 Litre 20W/50 Multigrade Motor Oil £3.99
M.O.T. TESTING 7 DAYS A WEEK
(Crossgates store only)
CHARLIE BROWNS CAR PART CENTRES
All offers valid until 18th October 1987 and are subject to availability at these stores only
Ring Road, Low Lane, Horsforth, Leeds. Tel: (0532) 584848
Kirkstall Road, Kirkstall, Leeds. Tel: (0532) 445261
642 York Road, Crossgates, Leeds. Tel: (0532) 645020
2 Commercial Road, off Bradford Road, Dewsbury. Tel. (0924) 465706
Northgate, Wakefield. Tel: (0924) 375533
OPEN 8AM-6PM MONDAY TO SATURDAY AND 10AM-4PM SUNDAYS

20 February 1987. Mrs Thatcher is all smiles as she tries her talents at machining a pocket lining for a jacket during her visit to Centaur Clothes, Great George Street, Leeds, during her day in Yorkshire yesterday. Miss Karen Pheasby, 19, who normally works on the machine, shows how it's done. Mr John Jackson, chairman and managing director of Centaur Clothes, is on the left.

Elland Road, Leeds, 22 February 1987. Isolated trouble broke out on the terrace...here a policeman collects helmets which were knocked off.

Leeds 2 April 1987. The notorious Woodpecker junction. Plans are in the pipeline to get something done and the bad news – it may be the end of the 1980s before the start is made.

Leeds, 17 April 1987. The 'Keep the Streets Neat' litter campaign is costing Leeds City Council £1 million. in new equipment including a fleet of 20 Street King cleaners – the latest thing in roadsweeping technology. Street cleaner Malcolm Gibb. *YEP* reporter Peter Anderson joined the roadsweeping nighshift in Leeds City Centre.

British Airways Concorde at Leeds Bradford Airport, 26 April 1987. A group of passengers.

Leeds, 3 May 1987. England and Manchester United captain Bryan Robson at Harehills Middle School, Leeds, where he presented the school football team with a complete strip donated by Wembley Sportsmaster Ltd and a soccer ball which he is seen handing over to team captain Donovan Daniel.

Leeds City Varieties: Britain's oldest theatre is going up for sale. This was announced today by the Joseph family, who have controlled the theatre for nearly 50 of its 225 year existence. It's co-director brothers Michael (right) and Stanley Joseph have placed sale notices in both Leeds and London newspapers for the 686-seat theatre, 11 May 1987.

Leeds, 28 July 1987. Genesis at Roundhay Park.

Leeds, 28 July 1987. Genesis at Roundhay Park.

Leeds, 28 July 1987. Genesis at Roundhay Park.

14 November 1987. This fire which broke out early in craft workshops at Allerton Grange High School, Moortown, Leeds, is believed to have started in a pottery kiln. Station officer Alan O'Neill said the classroom in which the fire started was fairly badly damaged.

WEST YORKSHIRE

Explosion and fire at Leeds University, 17 December 1987.

Salvation Army, Leeds 10 December 1987. The Salvation Army hostel in Lisbon Street, Leeds, is home for 68-year-old Eddie Wheelhouse.

Leeds, 28 September 1987. An appeal is going out to the thousands of couples who met before the war at the Dennis Altman School of Dancing, formerly the Mark Altman School, in Leeds. The dancing has continued through two world wars and 85 years. Mr Dennis Altman, the ex-Leeds councillor, who now heads the school in Great George Street, is hoping couples who met there will return for the birthday celebrations in November. 'In pre-war days dance halls were the only way boy could meet girl' he said. 'We had so many romances leading to engagements that we used to hold wedding receptions here. I hope a few of the couples who met in this way will get in touch. We have had to limit the numbers to 250 for comfort's sake. I had a phone call from an 86-year-old man who told me he came to a wedding reception here when he was six'.

Merrion Centre, Leeds, 1988.

Leeds, 13 January 1988. Mrs Betty Lee at work in the busy sterile supplies department at Leeds Infirmary.

17 January 1988, Leeds United's Bell's Manager of the Month Billy Bremner.

Chapeltown, Leeds 18 January 1988. Dusk, and another customer enters this Leeds sex shop.

Leeds, 2 March 1988. Fire at Leeds clothing warehouse on Roseville Road, Leeds. Rescue team (from left): David Moss, Derrick Harris, Darren Woods and Malcolm Wilson. They scaled scaffolding and helped people to escape as the blaze took hold.

30 March 1988. A car through the wall at Greek Street car park in Leeds City centre.

2 March 1988. Fire at Leeds clothing warehouse on Roseville Road.

ROSEVILLE ROAD

11 June 1988. Leeds based clothing design specialist Cimara Ltd has been awarded the contract to provide uniforms for this year's British Olympic team. Cimara will also be providing uniforms for the British team competing in the

Paralympics which take place in South Korea immediately after the Seoul Olympics. Cimaras's managing director (pictured with some of the staff) later became Councillor Mark Harris of Leeds City Council.

Leeds, 26 August 1988. Ice cream time for Vanessa Wright and Cheryl Daniel, both of Chapeltown.

Crossgates, Leeds, 1988. Arndale Shopping Centre during Christmas 1988.

Leeds, Headingley, December 1988. Six new executive boxes at the St Michael's Lane End of the famous ground.

Chapeltown, Leeds 1988. The West Indian Carnival.

9 August 1988. An unusual catch displayed at Leeds fish wholesalers Sea Harvest at Cross Green, Leeds. This blue marlin fish, which weighs 91lbs and is 7ft 4in long, was caught in salmon nets off North Shields. It is possibly the only fish of its kind to be caught in these waters in over a century. Looking over the fish are (right) Mr Jim Craig, co-owner of Sea Harvest and Mr Anthony Leck, the executive head chef at the Parkway Hotel, Leeds, where the fish will end up on the menu.

SEA
HARVE

The Hilton, Leeds, 2 December 1989.

Gordon Strachan after signing for Leeds United in 1989.

Leeds 26 January 1989. The landlord of Whitelocks, Briggate. Mr Fred Cliffe, right, and his wife Julia, receive the Campaign for Real Ales regional best pub of the year award.

Armley, Leeds, 24 March 1989. A friendly pet, easy to care for and with a personality all his own – Monty the 12ft python is up for sale because his owner is moving house. Mrs Alison Whitaker, of Cedar Mount, Armley, has been Monty's owner for almost three years.

The 1990s

Leeds United 1991, photocall. Left to right, back row: Bobby Davison, Chris Whyte, Gary McAllister, John Lukic, Mervyn Day, Peter Haddock, Lee Chapman, Rod Wallace. Middle row: Alan Sutton(Physio), Ray Wallace, Steve Hodge, Chris Fairclough, John McClelland, Mike Whitlow, Mel Sterland, Mick Hennigan(coach). Front Row: David Batty, Gary Speed, Imre Varadi, Howard Wilkinson (manager), Gordon Strachan, Tony Dorigo, Chris Kamara.

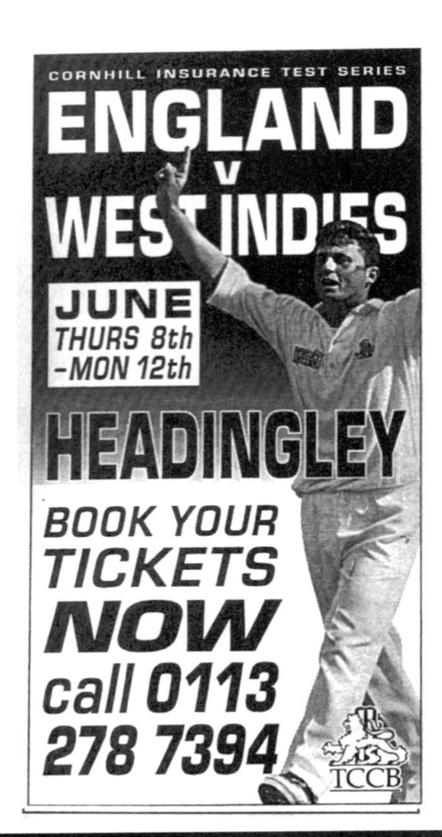

Guiseley, 2 April 1990. Salesmen at a Yorkshire factory have been given a new instruction by their boss – get knitting. From left: Bill Stewart, Bob McCulloch, Patrick Moody, Andrew Robinson and Lorinda Sheardby. Mr Patrick Moody, managing director of Wendy Wools, at Guiseley, Leeds, believes that it is time his 18-strong sales team learnt more about the product they sell worldwide – knitting wool. And he has bought in Featherstone's Gwen Matthewman, the world's fastest knitter, to provide the lessons. The crash course in knitting is under way and to prove that he really belives the experience will help his team, Mr Moody is taking part.

25 October 1990. Joiners Sam Roomes (left) and Jim Pembleton replace rotten wood in the roof of Thornton's Arcade, Leeds. The arcade is being carefully repaired and restored.

Leeds Theatres, Grand Theatre. October 1990. Banner waving protesters urged opera lovers to show their disapproval of controversial scenes during last night's first-night performance at the Grand Theatre, Leeds. As theatregoers arrived for the premiere of Opera North's *The Threepenny Opera* - featuring the song *Mac the Knife* – members of Friends of Opera North handed out protest leaflets. They say extra scenes are added which glorify sexual violence against women and want to have them cut.

The Leeds carnival was praised by the police for its good-humoured spirit, 27 August 1990.

Colton Village, 1990. A small boy sleeps through protests for a new school at the Colton Lane polling station in Leeds.

Leeds, 11 April 1991. Park Lane College. Adam Tucker, 19-year-old leader of the student's union who was expelled for passing a forged £10 note. Students are threatening sit ins and exam disruption unless management at Park Lane College reinstate their president. Mr Tucker has been 'conditionally expelled' from the college.

Adel, Leeds, 24 July 1991. Denis Mason Jones, artist.

Chapeltown, Leeds, 1991. Shop front and Sikh man.

Leeds, 19 February 1991. Film makers Milena Dragic and Janis Goodman use magazine cuttings to make household waste take on a new life as puppets in a film produced by the Leeds Animated Workshop.

17 July 1991. Howard Wilkinson, Jon Newsome, Tony Dorigo, Gordon Strachan Yorkshire Evening Post Sponsorship.

17 July 1991. Leeds United players and staff Bill Fotherby, Gordon Strachan, Howard Wilkinson, Tony Dorigo, Jon Newsome with Yorkshire Evening Post Sponsorship.

Leeds, Elland Road, 12 August 1991. Leeds United team group photograph showing the players and manager holding copies of the Yorkshire Evening Post.

EXIT
EXIT
Evening Post
UNITED SET FOR GLORY SEASON

YORKSHIRE Evening Post

SPONSORS OF LEEDS UNITED THE CHAMPIONS

Telephone Leeds 432701 Classified advertising 441234

SATURDAY 2 MAY 1992 25p

IT'S OURS!

Axe teachers plan 'callous'

A SHOCK cost cutting plan proposes to sever the education lifeline of chronically ill children by slashing the numbers of Leeds hospital teachers by two thirds.

But the Leeds Council Education Department cuts which propose a reduction in the numbers of Leeds hospital teachers from 16 to just five have been attacked as "callous" by the city's health watchdogs, paediatricians, teachers and their unions.

Dr Peter Dear, Clinical Director of Children's Services at St James's Hospital, Leeds, where the plan would cut the teaching staff to just one teacher said: "We are very concerned about these proposals. We have large numbers of children in this hospital needing long term treatment and an education is vital."

Coun Keith Burnley, chairman of Leeds Education Committee, said: "These proposals will be considered in committee on May 6 and May 11. The intention is efficiency and to save money by delivering the service differently."

Ticket touts war declared

THE threat of life bans from Elland Road was today hanging over "so called Leeds United supporters" who have sold tickets for this afternoon's match to touts.

The club was mounting a major undercover operation to buy tickets from touts operating outside the ground.

Tickets bought by club representatives, posing as fans desperate to get into the game, were being traced to their original purchaser via the club's computerised ticket system.

● An arson attack hit the main stand and part of the pitch at Wolverhampton Wanderers' Molineux ground today, but the club's Second Division fixture against Middlesbrough was going ahead as planned.

Boy in canal death plunge

SCREAMING children raised the alarm after an 11-year-old boy plunged from a bridge into the freezing water of a North Yorkshire canal and drowned.

Youngsters ran to the nearby Selby Fire Station for help after David Stephen Welsh fell 30 feet from the bridge carrying the Selby-Bawtry road while he was playing with his brother Andrew, 10.

David attended the Holy Family School in Carlton, Selby.

Guard hurt in van robbery

TWO men attacked the crew of a security van in Leeds today, injuring a security guard and escaping with a cash box.

The robbery happened outside the post office at the Seacroft Centre at 11 am today.

The raiders fled in a grey Ford Sierra, Reg No E535 VWT, which had been stolen yesterday from the car park of a city hospital.

THE *Yorkshire Evening Post* will be published as usual on May Day Monday, packed with reports and pictures of the momentous achievements of Leeds United and the city's celebrations over the weekend of their League Championship victory.

This historic occasion will mean a *Yorkshire Evening Post* that no reader can afford to miss.

So make sure of YOUR copy on Monday.

▲ LET'S CELEBRATE...United's victorious squad, with the League Championship trophy, at Elland Road this afternoon. MIKE COWLING

Picture that says 'We are the Champions'

By DON WARTERS

IT was carnival time at Elland Road this afternoon as a sell-out crowd, in party mood, celebrated Leeds United's achievement in winning the First Division Championship.

The celebrations started early as joyous fans waited for the League Championship trophy to be presented.

The *Yorkshire Evening Post* Brass Band entertained, the Mexican wave swept around the ground, and balloons in blue and gold blew around the stadium.

Understandably there was a tremendous roar when the United side, sponsored by the *Yorkshire Evening Post*, were brought out onto the pitch for the presentation.

Club chairman Leslie Silver was presented with a Barclays League cheque for £100,000, the prize for winning the title, and then manager Howard Wilkinson was handed a bottle of champagne.

Then the moment all Leeds fans had been waiting for arrived when skipper Gordon Strachan received the 104-year-old League Championship trophy.

Leeds fans roared their approval and chanted "Are You Watching Manchester".

The trophy was then passed down the line and every member of the United squad had his turn at holding the trophy as a battery of Press photographers clicked merrily away.

The match which was to follow seemed almost incidental but there was 90 minutes football still to get through and United were defending an unbeaten home League record.

★A full match report will appear in our *Football Results Extra* on sale later this evening.

Yorkshire Evening Post Saturday 2 May 1992. Leeds United Championship winning Paper.

YORKSHIRE Evening Post

Telephone Leeds 432701 Classified advertising 441234

SATURDAY 2 MAY 1992 25p

CHAMPIONS!

A SUPERB SOUVENIR OF THE DAY THE FOOTBALL LEAGUE CROWN CAME BACK TO LEEDS

Yorkshire Evening Post Saturday 2 May 1992. Leeds United Championship winning supplement.

Leeds United on their open-top bus tour after winning the First Division title in 1992.

Leeds United League champions 1992. Howard Wilkinson with the trophy, 3 May 1992.

Fans celebrate after the title-winning match --Leeds United v Sheffield United, 26 April 1992.

Leeds United 1992 League champions. From left: Carl Shutt (slightly obscured), Gary Speed, Gordon Strachan, Chris Fairclough (behind Strachan). Mel Sterland (behind trophy), John Lukic and Jon Newsome.

Richard and Janice Morley have received the *Yorkshire Evening Post* classified Best Pub of the Year Award for the second year running for their pub The Travellers Rest at Crossgates, Leeds, 12 November 1992.

Leeds, 16 June 1992. Past master Geoff Boycott and latter-day genius Sachin Tendulkar give Lord Mayor of Leeds Councillor Denise Atkinson one or two tips on the art of batting.

Leeds, Roundhay, 17 August 1992. Michael Jackson concert.

Leeds, 22 October 1992. Tyrannosaurus Rex stalks the Tropical World at Roundhay Park with 13 of his friends. And waking them up at the Dinosaurs Alive! exhibition is seven-year-old Gareth Kitchen of Turton Green, Gildersome. He won a *Yorkshire Evening Post* competition to open the exhibition.

Chapeltown, Leeds, 1993. Youth Project.

Leeds, 15 February 1993. Actor Jon Pertwee at the Schofield Centre, Leeds, with Wayne Kaeey, 7, of Gipton, and Christopher Cunningham, 4, of Moortown. The boys, winners of a Worzel Gummidge lookalike competition, had been hoping to meet TV scarecrow Mr Pertwee during his visit to the city in August but were disappointed when he fell ill and had to cut short his stay.

Leeds Cinemas. The Odeon cinema on the corner New Briggate and The Headrow, March 1993.

Princess Diana meets crowds during a walkabout in Leeds after visiting Leeds Relate Centre in 1993.

Queens Hotel Leeds. Queen's. City Square. Commissionaire Kelly Sutton. 1993.

Princess Diana in Leeds in April 1993.

Leeds Cinemas. The Hyde Park Picture House, Brudenell Road, Leeds. Pictured in June 1993 are Liz Rymer, manager, and Geoff Thompson, former owner.

Chapeltown Leeds 2 June 1993. Police on standby off Chapeltown Road.

Hunslet, Leeds, 12 November 1993. Pupils of St Mary's Primary School enjoy a game of hopscotch as they celebrate the school's 50th anniversary. From the left are: Matthew Laycock, nine, Michael Graham, five, Sarah Howard, 11, and Suzanne Hullah, eight. They were among children and teachers who donned Victorian costumes for the day and were presented with special mugs designed by Leeds Development Corporation. Stuart Kenny, director of development and marketing for the LDC, said 1943 was an important year for Hunlset, but this year would be better, with the start of the Hunslet Green Development.

Rail crash at Leeds City Station, November 1993.

Leeds, Seacroft, 3 August 1993. Seacroft shopping centre.

Leeds City Varieties: Old theatres reek of powerful emotion. Although wary of talking about seeing ghosts, stage manager Jason Salvin, during a break in dress rehearsals for Dick Whittington, was happy to admit he had encountered presences and auras in many parts of the old theatre, 17 December 1993.

Leeds, 20 November 1993. Simon Young, abseiling down the Town Hall's clock tower, aiming to raise public awareness of local youth activity.

Granary Wharf, Leeds. In the background Leeds City Station and to the right the Hilton Hotel in 1994.

Duncan Street, Leeds, 31 May 1994. New Market Street junction.

Leeds, 8 July 1994. Young artists: From left, Chris Leach, Rosie Harris, Katherine Round and Jenny Baker.

Temple Newsam, Leeds, 17 July 1994. One of the soloists, Keith Latham, is pictured during his performace at the Opera in the Park.

The entrance to the new National Express bus station at Dyer Street, 1996.

Visitors to Granary Wharf, Leeds, yesterday (Sunday) were treated to the sound of Samba music, when a touch of Rio came to the city. Granary Wharf held a Carnaval (not carnival) for the visitors and in the picture Danny Henry of the Leeds and Bradford Samba Bands is seen here entertaining the visitors, 1996.

The new Leeds City Bus Station, 1996.

Tony Blair delivers his speech at the North and Yorkshire Business Forum at the Royal Armouries, Leeds .

The new White Rose Centre in Leeds.

City of Leeds-sponsored swordfish bi-plane takes to the skies at Leeds Bradford airport on a visit.

Leeds
Bradford
Airport

Pollution Story. Traffic on Westgate flyover.

Smog over Leeds viewed along Scott Hall Road, 1997.

Building work in progress on the Norwich Union site at City Square, Leeds in 1996.

No.1 City Square in the centre of Leeds. The new office block of Norwich Union, 1997.

Leeds Clubscene. The imposing frontage of the Majestyk club, City Square in 1996.

The North Mall at the new White Rose Centre, Leeds.

The main entrance nears completion at the new White Rose Centre, Leeds.

The Central Atrium in the upper level at the new White Rose Centre.

Shoppers in the mall at the White Rose Shopping Centre, which opened to the public for the first time on 25 March 1997.

Star Wars trilogy opens at the Odeon cinema, Leeds city centre, with queues stretching down the Headrow, 1997.

Amazed shoppers get a rare chance to see members of the Othokela Ngoma Zulu dance group, from the Kwazulu-Natal region of South Africa, performing their traditional tribal steps when they visited the Victoria Quarter in Leeds, 1997.

John Major pictured speaking to pupils of the Leeds Grammar School on Monday 21 April 1997.

All roads lead to the city as dusk falls over Leeds and traffic follows cones left by workmen at the end of the M1, 1997.

The main entrance at the new Leeds Grammar School site at Alwoodley.

All change...Traffic being diverted on the Vicar Lane, Leeds, as the new traffic system is put into operation, 1997.

New suspension footbridge acrossing the new M1/M621 link road in Leeds, 1997.

U2 stage construction at Roundhay Park, Leeds, 1997.

Benjie Ziff, 10, arrives for his first day at the new Leeds Grammar School.

Traffic congestion on the M621, in Leeds, due to road work delays, 1997.

A homeless person who will not be having a Happy Christmas asleep in a doorway on Wellington Street, Leeds, as shoppers walk by oblivious, 1995.

Traffic on 14 January 1998.

Crashed Leeds United plane on runway at Stansted Airport London.

View across Leeds. Pictured centre is the new DHSS building (Quarry House), 1998.

The main stage in the shadow of Temple Newsam at The Leeds '99 Festival.

MEAN FIDDLER
PRESENTS
LEEDS
MEAN FIDDLER
PRESENTS
LEEDS
S·U·B
P·O·P

A new style articulated 'bendy' bus is photographed in City Square during a visit to Leeds, 1999.

Royal Mail building in Wellington Street, Leeds, is up for sale.

Royal Marine Commandos abseiled down the offices of Railtrack in City Square, Leeds, unveiling banners to launch to £165 million project for Leeds City Station, 1999.

Picture from the roof of West Riding House, Albion Street, Leeds. One of the biggest buildings to be found in Leeds is Quarry House. Dominating the eastern gateway to the city, the building takes its name from the site of former flats that once stood in the area.

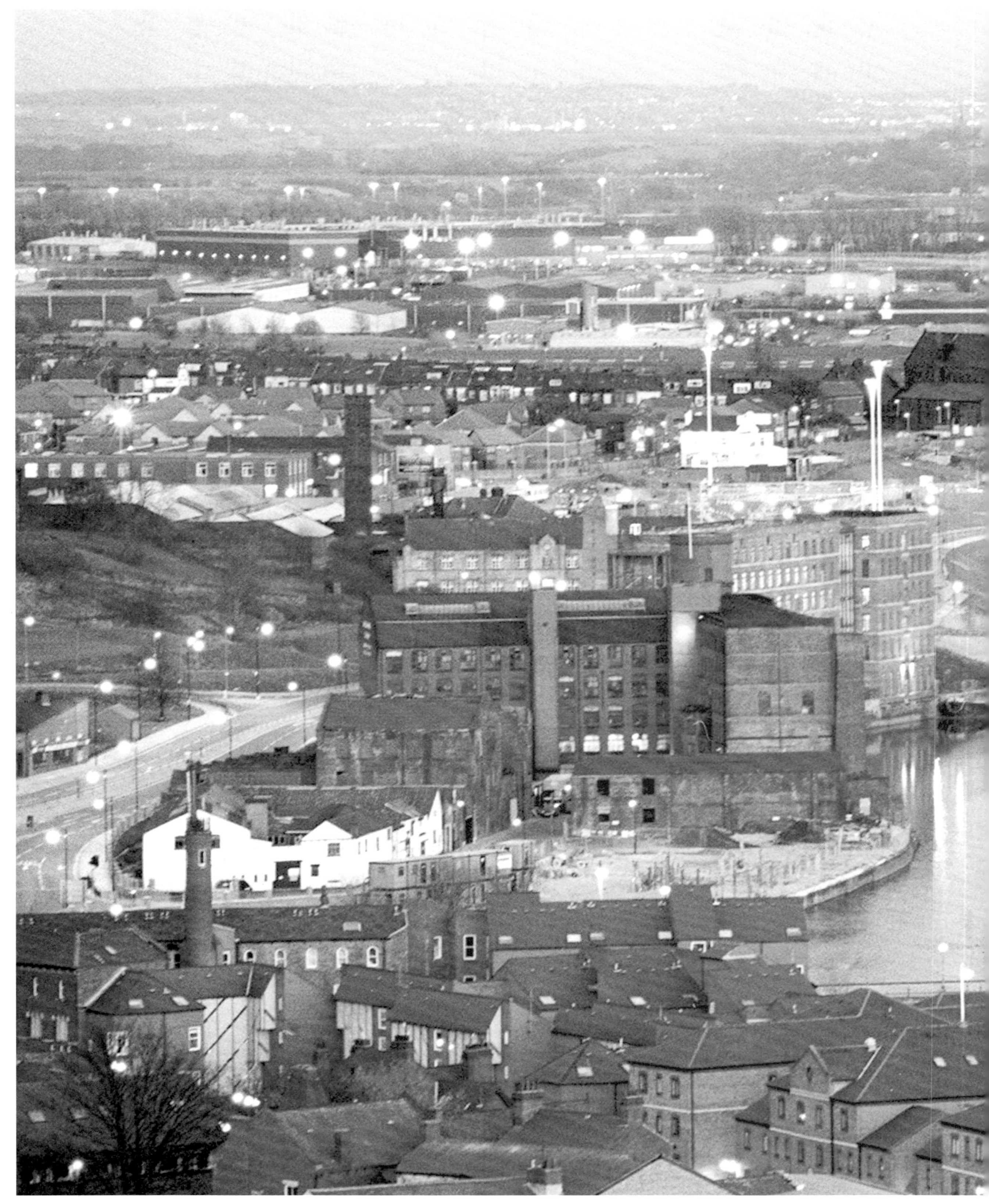

Picture from the roof of West Riding House, Albion Street, Leeds. The old and the new in building design face each other across a stretch of water used in the booming period of the history of Leeds. The Royal Armouries to the right

and old mills and warehouses to the left contine to be reflected in the canal.

Cars parked on Wesley Street and Stadium Way during the live televising of the Manchester United v Leeds United game at Elland Road, 1999.

Lord Mayor of Leeds Councillor Keith Parker puts a light to the Victoria Square beacon.

1999, heavy traffic on Churwell Hill, Churwell.

1997, construction work at Leeds Rhinos stadium, Headingley, Leeds.